CONTENTS

CHAPTER 1

BELLE OF
Louisville

A sailor on the *Belle of Louisville* was writing in his **log**. Suddenly he felt cold. He turned around. He thought he saw a strange man behind him. He was frightened. It looked like the ghost of Ben Winters.

Throughout history sailors have often written in logs and on maps. It is a way to record their journeys.

5

Winters had become the captain of the *Belle* in 1947. He thought he was above the law. Winters let illegal betting take place. So police attacked the ship in 1948. Winters died during the **raid**. But many people believe they see his ghost.

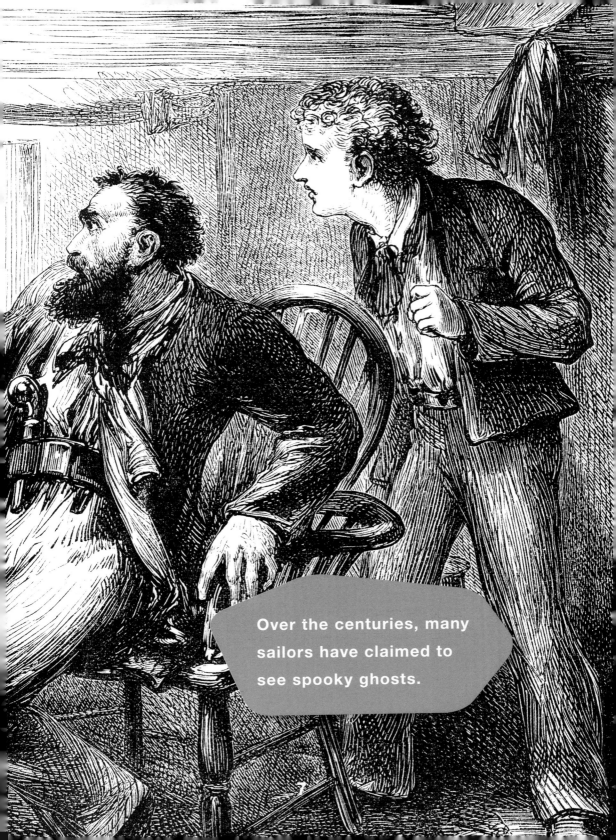

Over the centuries, many sailors have claimed to see spooky ghosts.

Ghosts might **haunt** ships around the world. The *Belle* is one of them. This **steamboat** has had many names. It was first called *Idlewild*. Then it was named *Avalon*. It became the *Belle of Louisville* in 1963. Sailors say it is bad luck to give ships new names. Some people believe this is why the ship is haunted.

STILL AFLOAT

The *Belle* still carries passengers. It docks in Louisville, Kentucky, USA.

The *Belle* is the oldest running steamboat of its kind in the world.

BELLE of LOUISVILLE

CHAPTER 2

FLYING
Dutchman

People believe the *Flying Dutchman* still haunts the oceans. Long ago this ship carried spices around the world. Its captain was Hendrick van der Decken. He was known for his fast sailing. Sailors thought he made deals with the devil for speed.

The *Flying Dutchman* sailed through a lot of bad weather.

11

Some people see a red glow around the *Dutchman*. Others say it is green.

Most captains fear storms. But bad weather did not scare van der Decken. In 1641, a storm near Africa was too rough. The *Dutchman* sank. Everyone on board died.

Sailors believe the ship was cursed to sail for all time. People still claim to see it and its ghostly captain. They say the ship has a glowing light around it. The ship is said to bring bad luck to anyone who spots it.

CURSED!

One legend says van der Decken's ghost is cursed. He can only walk on land every seven years. But he can break the curse. He must win the love of a woman.

CHAPTER 3

STAR OF
India

The *Star of India* has a troubled history. The ship made its first trip in 1863. It sailed from Liverpool, hoping to get to India. The ship crashed near Wales. Then it had a **mutiny**.

The *Star of India* was one of the first ships to be made of iron instead of wood.

The ship's second trip was even worse. It was damaged in a storm. The captain died on board.

The ghost of a young **stowaway** might haunt the ship. His name was John Campbell. The new captain put Campbell to work. Campbell climbed a **mast**. He slipped. He fell 30 metres (100 feet) to the deck and died.

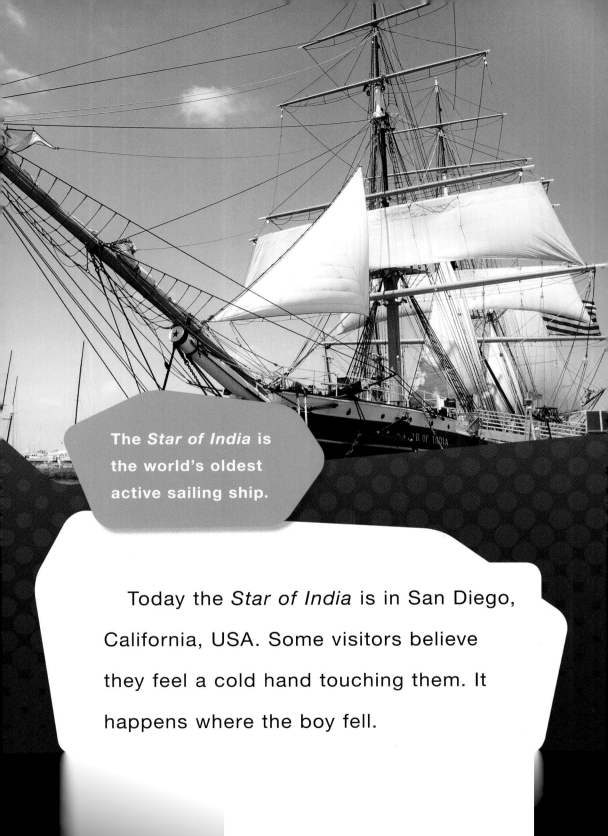

The *Star of India* is the world's oldest active sailing ship.

Today the *Star of India* is in San Diego, California, USA. Some visitors believe they feel a cold hand touching them. It happens where the boy fell.

CHAPTER 4

QUEEN
Mary

The *Queen Mary* sailed for 31 years. It carried people across the Atlantic Ocean. Today the ship is in Long Beach, California, USA. People say it is haunted.

Visitors to the *Queen Mary* can even stay overnight at the onboard hotel.

The *Queen Mary* was voted one of the Top 10 Most Haunted Places in America by *Time* magazine.

Many people have died on the ship. Some were crew members. Others were passengers. Sailor John Pedder was killed in 1966 in an accident. He was crushed by a door. A girl named Jackie also died. She drowned in a swimming pool.

Today some visitors say they hear a child laughing. But no one is there. Other people see Pedder's ghost in the engine room. Many visitors ask about the ghosts. Ship visitors can even go on ghost tours.

CHAPTER 5

USS Constitution

Workers on the USS *Constitution* do not joke about ghosts. They believe that stories about the warship are real. People come from far away to visit the ship. It is in Boston, Massachusetts, USA.

The USS *Constitution* is often called Old Ironsides because it was such a strong ship.

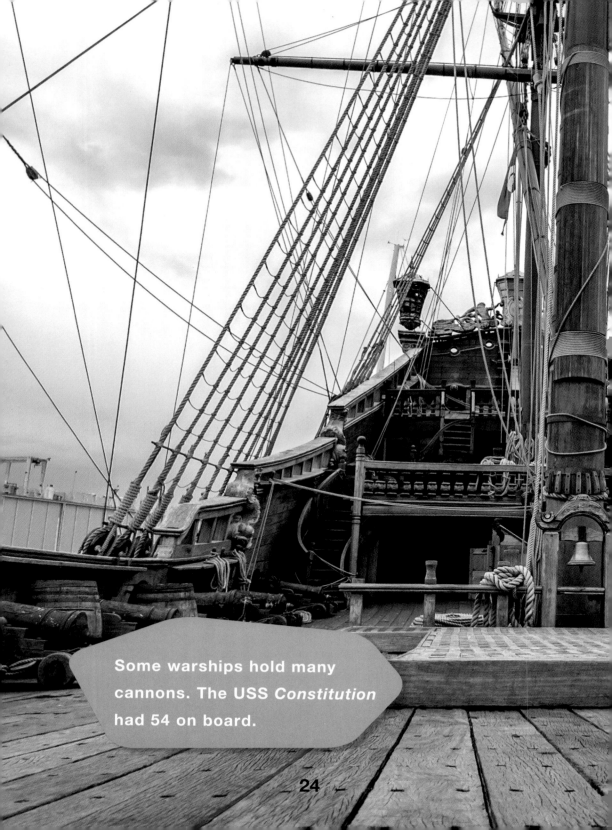

Some warships hold many cannons. The USS *Constitution* had 54 on board.

The *Constitution* only sails on special days now. But strange things still happen. Sometimes a **cannonball** rolls across the deck. People do not know why it happens.

Sometimes people see ghosts on ships as shadowy figures. Other times people see ghosts covered in blood.

One night four crew members thought they saw a ghost. It was a man. He was wearing a dark jacket with gold buttons. He had blood on his face and clothes. He quickly disappeared.

NO BIRDS HERE

Birds often land on ships. But crew members say birds are afraid to land on the USS *Constitution*.

GLOSSARY

cannonball
a heavy, round piece of metal that was fired from a cannon during wartime

haunt
to visit as a ghost

log
a record of a ship's journey

mast
a tall post on a ship that holds sails

mutiny
a rebellion by sailors against their ship's captain

raid
an attack by law enforcement to identify illegal items or practices

steamboat
a boat that is powered by a steam engine

stowaway
a person who hides aboard a ship without paying for passage

TRIVIA

1. People see the *Flying Dutchman* on both water and land. In 1939 people on a beach in South Africa saw it. It sailed towards them. Then it disappeared.

2. A man died while working below the deck of the *Star of India*. Other crew members did not realize he was there. They began raising the anchor. It made a loud noise. No one heard the man's screams. The anchor crushed him. It is said that his ghost still haunts the ship.

3. The last night watchman of the USS *Constitution* died in 1963. Some visitors have seen his ghost play cards on the lower deck of the ship.

ACTIVITY

Write a short play about one of the haunted ships mentioned in this book. Imagine that your characters are crew members on the ship who meet one of the ghosts. What do the crew members see? How do they react? Include spooky information about how the ghost looks and sounds. Add details about other strange events that happen on the ship too.

FIND OUT MORE

Books

Frightful Ghost Ships, James Roland (Lerner Publications, 2017)

Ghost Ships (Unexplained Mysteries), Lisa Owings (Epic, 2015)

RMS Queen Mary (Scariest Places on Earth), Michael Ferut (Bellweather Media, 2015)

Websites

Star of India Maritime Museum of San Diego: sdmaritime.org/visit/the-ships/star-of-india/

Stories of ghost ships: www.livescience.com/48489-tales-of-ghost-ships.html

USS Constitution Museum: ussconstitutionmuseum.org/

INDEX